2·95

DRIVING HOME

Poems New and Selected

D1318320

Miriam Waddington

TORONTO
OXFORD UNIVERSITY PRESS
1972

FOR VIRGINIA P. ROBINSON

The poems in the second section have been selected from *Green World* (1945), *The Second Silence* (1955), *The Season's Lovers* (1958), *The Glass Trumpet* (1966), *Call Them Canadians* (1968), *Say Yes* (1969). The new poems have appeared in *Canadian Literature, English* (London), *Far Point, Impulse, Journal of Canadian Studies, Malahat Review, Midstream, New, New Measure* (London), *Poetry Review* (London), *Queen's Quarterly, Saturday Night, Viewpoints, Wascana Review, West Coast Review*.

The author and publisher wish to acknowledge the assistance of
The Canada Council

ISBN 0-19-540200-6

© Oxford University Press (Canadian Branch) 1972

1 2 3 4 — 5 4 3 2

Printed in Canada by
John Deyell Limited

Contents

NEW POEMS

CONTENTS

SELECTED POEMS

CONTENTS

CONTENTS

New Poems

Voyagers

This is my last song
to you, I am getting
ready to leave to
learn a new language
to accept my fate
of ten provinces and
the junction of two
rivers, something small
poor with not many
people and a lot of
dry silence

but bless me as I
bless you and remember
our oceans
remember our continents
don't ever forget
Henry Hudson
adrift
in his birchbark canoe

Transformations

The blood of my ancestors
has died in me
I have forsaken the steppes
of Russia for the prairies
of Winnipeg, I have turned
my back on Minneapolis
and the Detroit lakes
I love only St. Boniface
its grey wooden churches
I want to spend my life
in Gimli listening to the
roar of emptiness in the
wild snow, scanning the lake
for the music of rainbow-
skinned fishes, I will compose
my songs to gold-eye tunes
send them across the land
in smoke-spaces, ice-signals
and concentrate all winter
on Henry Hudson adrift
in a boat, when he comes home
I will come home too and
the blood of my ancestors
will flower on Mennonite bushes

Signs

1
there is something
pure absolute and
unbreakable in you
it will last
a thousand years
I don't know why
it breaks my
heart but
it does

2
an Indian word
is carved on
a 2000-year-old
glacial stone
in Manitoba
that message
I read in your
face

it is a
discovery and
it scares me

3
I could have
lived without
those glacial
messages
those lakes
of cold laughter

4
maybe you are
eternal
a myth of wind
in the
Alberta foothills
the dark-bearded
man:
yes or no
the sea will be
my murderer

5
I don't mind
because you will
live a thousand
years
you will stand
on the shore
of Labrador a
storyteller
your words will
greet everyone
who comes and

I'll hear them too

A landscape of
John Sutherland

we are
in flight
we are
a space of
dreamed-of
light
autumn canyons
crevices
we are the blue
between
the sliding doors
of sky

we fall
among the shells
the molluscs
of our concerts
on the earth
our bones
are toys
and trumpets
for the wind
our song
sand
on a shore

our eyes
are owls
who scold
the lit-up
winter night,
our skeletons

snow animals
who prowl
through the
quiet moment
of landscape

that is
what I like
best, to find
the quiet moment
shadowless
in the roar
of landscape
to be the
landscape

Origins

The great bonesetter
is mute his hands
alone speak for him
his tongue stumbles
over words
the rocky barriers
melt under his touch
disconnected things
connect sea and rockface
obliterate all traces

I wish my life
was a movie

I wish my life
was a movie
by Jean-Luc Godard
then I could be
always
twelve years old
riding my bicycle
to school chased
by cops & robbers
pursued by Italian
lovers & evil
uncles haunted by
cemeteries with
false fronts &
all those innocent
bystanders who are
still waiting
trussed-up & gagged
in the wooden cupboards
of suburban
apartments in Paris
for the legendary
war to end

Every Tuesday
would be a historic
holiday in the
annals of revolution
every citizen would
change to clean white
socks & every subway
stop would be
absolutely the

very last one where
fantasy & reality
would get off
together & walk away
arm in arm fickle
as my schoolgirl
attachments but just
as eternal just as
monumental & just
as interchangeable

The world on Easter morning

The Thames is choked with daffodils
and Abraham's bridge is falling down,
from Golder's Green to Whitechapel
the music of the festivals
drowns in traffic-stars and bells:
red rover red rover we call you all over!
The desert bleeds into the sea
and the little white lambs of Passover
skip startled over Hampstead Heath
where Judah's lion is tumbling down
and a wounded world is limping home
from the cold Red River to Galilee
all on an Easter morning.

Between cities

The boughs
of winter
sleep under
a floor of
broken snow
and frost
sings in
the temples
of Jerusalem.

Your face
burns with
the fire of
lost cities
I study it
in line and
legend in all
its mountainous
leaning, I learn
its ancient
burials its
white valleys.

And I shuffle
my visions
revise my
prophecies, see
through the
tentless sky
words golden
as rooftops
fresh buttery
as daffodils

(I'm in a
country of
miracles a
forest-path
on a biblical
expressway)

I unroll run
for miles, travel
to everywhere
with your eye's
document; hang,
balance, stretch—
bind the endless
snows in desert
granaries and
look your smile
dissolves the
rockbound lines
of distance.

Eavesdropping

I live in the drawer
of an empty bureau
in one of the rooms
in my house in Toronto,
when the telephone rings
I spy on myself, I wonder
who is telephoning me
when I'm not even here,
when I've gone to
London (except that
I've really stayed
here folded away
in this empty drawer).

Maybe someone is calling
to say: your last book
was a runaway bestseller
you're famous and you're
going to get 15% net
in royalties and a Governor
General's medal and
you can retire on the
movie rights and

You can be a full
professor at last, maybe
a resident poet, take it
easy, go on exchange
to a college in California
eat breakfast on the
terrace in January and get
two years tax exemption.

You can be in
Who's Who this year
next year and last
year and have students
writing you respectful
letters: dear Professor
Waddington what is your
frank opinion of other
Canadian poets?

Or maybe it's that man
from Chicago telephoning
at last to ask me to
dinner to say how he
can't live without me
another minute and
can we please be
happily ever after?

But the telephone
keeps on ringing and
I know if I answer it
it will only be the
insurance adjuster
saying: your car is
a total wreck madam
but not a complete
write-off so what
do you want us to do
about it?

And if it's him
the insurance adjuster
my answer is: call me
next week when I have
more time *come to me*
when you're old come
to me when you need
coffee but for now
can't you see I'm
busy, can't you see I'm
living in the empty
drawer of this bureau
where I can close my
eyes and see the
scarlet climbers?

Where I can remember
that some roses have
no smell, others no
colour, but that's nice
too when I'm trying
to go to sleep in the
brown wooden lining
of this medium-sized
drawer in the medium-
warm month of June which
is too medium a season
for trying to fit
myself into being
this new small size
from now on.

Lights

In Toronto
a clutch of
swinging doors
a growing nest
of stone birds
the tremble of the
path of a water-
bug in a drowned
river.

Under my stone
hand the falling
towers of Avignon:
blood brickdust
and the roofless
skies above Sicilian
orchards are pressing
on layered subway
tunnels the white
seeds of their
pomegranate cities.

I am the black
Arctic and the poison
cold the paralyzed
grove of lighted
birch the sled
of the dog-star
pulling the sky
across the Canadas
I am the branches
of my own arms
the many-mothered
lullaby where
my baby country
still sleeps.

The nineteen thirties are over

The nineteen thirties
are over; we survived
the depression, the Sacco-
Vanzetti of childhood
saw Tom Mooney smiling
at us from photographs,
put a rose on the grave
of Eugene Debs, listened
to our father's stories
of the Winnipeg strike and
joined the study groups
of the OBU always keeping
one eye on the revolution.

Later we played records
with thorn needles, Josh
White's *Talking Union* and
Prokofief's *Lieutenant Kije,*
shuddered at the sound of
bells and all those wolves
whirling past us in snow
on the corner of Portage
and Main, but in my mind
summer never ended on the
shores of Gimli where we
looked across to an Icelandic
paradise we could never see
the other side of; and I
dreamed of Mexico and shining
birds who beckoned to me
from the gold-braided lianas
of my own wonder.

These days I step out
from the frame of my wind-
battered house into Toronto
city; somewhere I still
celebrate sunlight, touch
the rose on the grave of
Eugene Debs but I walk
carefully in this land
of sooty snow; I pass the
rich houses and double
garages and I am not really
this middle-aged professor
but someone from
Winnipeg whose bones ache
with the broken revolutions
of Europe, and even now
I am standing on the heaving
ploughed-up field
of my father's old war.

Fence post

When spring left town
I was busy addressing
envelopes and I didn't
notice; I scarcely
looked up from my desk
when the procession
passed by taking summer
to the station; then
autumn went south and
all of a sudden the boys
I used to go around with
were sixty years old and
telling me money
isn't everything.

I didn't notice when
the fence-post in
the backyard grew
black with winter;
now its fine lines
and wires are everywhere
scratching the air
protesting against the
sky and I am a sheet
of snow wrapped in
snow blowing in the wind
not saying a word
because words don't
count and I have sworn

never to talk about
monsters never to tell
my dreams and the
ice verticals lie

across my heart with
perfect precision
some marvellous artist
has measured them out
and laid them there
and I can't help being
lost in admiration
for the weightless way
he is managing everything
especially my death.

Moscow roses

You send me roses
from Moscow a
postcard telling
about winter and
being stranded in
a hotel far from
the apple market.

You remind me
to feel helpless
and suddenly I'm
surrounded by
empty fur coats
who have lost
the people who
used to wear them.

Advice to the young

1
Keep bees and
grow asparagus,
watch the tides
and listen to the
wind instead of
the politicians
make up your own
stories and believe
them if you want to
live the good life.

2
All rituals
are instincts
never fully
trust them but
study to im-
prove biology
with reason.

3
Digging trenches
for asparagus
is good for the
muscles and
waiting for the
plants to settle
teaches patience
to those who are
usually in too
much of a hurry.

4

There is morality
in bee-keeping
it teaches how
not to be afraid
of the bee swarm
it teaches how
not to be afraid of
finding new places
and building in them
all over again.

Song: Elijah

Elijah's gone to Poland
as naked as William Blake,
his beard is as black as a chimney
his eyes are a Baltic lake.

He sifts the mounds of rubble,
broken bottles and lead,
Elijah counts his children,
his Warsaw children are dead.

The Jewish *seder* is over,
Jerusalem's song is still,
Poland spills with echoes—
but Elijah's beaker is full

Of night as black as the chimneys
and the wailing of William Blake,
Elijah sits in Poland
and sips his own heartbreak.

Why should I care
about the world

Gone is
the holiness
in where I
lived, my song.

Why should I care
what happens to
the world why
should I
broodingly
seek the cell of
holiness the
habit in where
I lived, my song?

(Your song
was only a few
ragged Scotsmen
in Kildonan, some
riff-raffy settlers,
half-breeds, Indians,
Galician labourers,
scraggly-ended
pee-smelling prairie
towns)

(it was a flat
stony mound
for a mountain
a silly tuft
of pine on
an island in
Lac du Bonnet,
berry-picking in a

buffalo summer
beside a wheat ocean
and jumping the
ditches brimming
with rain.)

Gone now; all
cracked open like
eggs at Easter
parted like three
feathers in a
bird's tail of wind.

And I can't even
go back to being
dirty Jew, to
hearing from the
conductor on the
Selkirk streetcar:
your father is
a Bolshevik isn't
he little girl?

This is a very
far very long
way to be away
from the holiness
in where I lived
my song.

Sad winter in
the land of Can. Lit.

I tell myself
I am sad because
it is winter:
but Nelly Sachs
lived through
many such winters
and poured biblical
summer through the
blackest chimneys.

Madame Nathalie
lived through them
too; she comes from
Moscow like my
grandmother and now
she will visit
Toronto and speak
to us in English.
Will I learn
anything from her?

There are many
things I must learn
in order to write
better in Canada.
I must learn to
write & for *and*
and *wll* for *will*:
to put : at the
beginning of a line
instead of at the end;
to spell everything
my own swt way just
to prve my indep
endens of all thr
shtty authrty.

I must learn to
write about dead
horses with myths
in my mouth, dead
birds and frogs
that I shot with
tears in my eyes
but compassion in
my heart just
because I'm human
and was born to
original sin.

I must learn to
sing the joy of
penises and all
their frequencies;
the gloriousness
of blow jobs and
how avant garde
is everything in
London Ontario;
they will then
maybe mistake me
for a 26-year-old
white-protestant-
anglo-saxon-or-
duddy-kravitz-ok-
type-jew—a man—or
someone who at least
reads comic books
and was once a cree
indian or a wistful
eskimo.

Dear Nelly Sachs,
dear Nathalie Sarraute,
isn't there anything
you can teach me
about how to write
better in Canada?

Language as I
used to believe in it

Why can't I be
satisfied
with images
out of language
as I used
to believe
in it?

why can't I say
your hair is black
as a raven's wing
your forehead
white as milk
your kiss cold,
the west wind?

(ordinary to say
your hair is black
as the raven's wing,
empty to say
your forehead
is white as milk,
your kisses cold)

(meaningless as
shining floors,
salads composed
at six o'clock
the clatter of
cutlery in kitchens
or the CBC news
at suppertime)

(dead as
the angling crane
flying over piles
of rubble beside
the humanities
building, but
clever, that fishing
in the fissures
of space; accurate
that dipping of
rods for bricks
to put up a library)

(so why do I think
of the wooden houses
of Moscow when your
name is a wilderness
I never intended
to get lost in?
I hold on to
the light I swing
on its thinnest
bars)

your touch maybe
is a clearing
in this desert of
books but your
hand is a nagging
wind ruffling
my notions of
order and I
remember your
kisses

looking out now
across dark lawns
to the lighted frames
of buildings
beside empty
parking lots and
I wonder

why I can't be
satisfied
with images
out of language
as I used to
believe in it
why I can't love
ravens' wings,
milkiness, what's
this passion
for clarity and

why do I think
of a dog with
bent ears a barn
in Manitoba
a hairy pulse
striking
the exact time
of night?

Song for sleeping people

Did you know
America is tilted
like a saucer, on
one side is Persia
on the other is
the moon and
America see-saws
between the two
and in the saucer
swim a million
coloured beads.
Butterflies slice
through the painted
flowers and children
run around the rim
of the saucer and
pick packets of
flower seeds, blue
forget-me-nots
to throw at the
moon, and I step
very light on the
rim of the saucer
I don't want to
make a noise, crack
the surface or
break anything
and I don't want
to wake up the
sleeping people
because one of them
might be me.

Polemics

I am not interested
in the polemics of art
you can keep your cosmic
gossip I don't care if
poetry is dying if the
language is debased if
you stuff people's ears
with bananas and their
mouths with dead elm
trees; to hell with style!
I'm in favour of living
I reject dying while
I'm still alive I don't
want to analyse the process
of how we disappear from
the world; I care only
how we appear; I want
to build apparitions
a million monuments
to the future completely
uncool, to shout from
the rooftops: *history
is not so fleeting!*
There were heroes, wars
were halted, men were
healed, children were
born, people sang,
worlds were changed;
I don't want to be ashamed
of the word *courage* or
choke on the word *love*
or deny the category
of being human any more;
I want to say *brother* and

see when I close my eyes
not ploughs of riot or
fields of burning people
or the bones of smoking
cities: I want to see
vistas of all that is
being made impossible—
civilization.

Anxious

Anxious
of course I'm anxious
afraid
of course I'm afraid
I don't know what about
I don't know what of
but I'm afraid
and I feel it's
right to be.

In small towns

Unreal as the
shifting fields
of winter
was your crossing
my threshold;
it must have been
in a dream dreamed
by children that
you came very
imaginative light
and delicate; fitful;
not at all like
those prairie towns
we lived in or maybe
yes, delicate like them
in a landscape of ink
and flat paper
all those fastidious
township plans and
lot surveys penned
through with paths
leading to the very edge
of maps dwindling
into distant archives.

It is all managed
with tentative lines
sketching the future
speculating about
the past, it is done
with apparitions
of sixteen-year-olds
finding themselves

suddenly in the
Silver Slipper Café
surfacing sharply
from a haze of
lost times in
the small towns
of Manitoba.

Imitations

I wish I were
a dog asleep
in the orchards
of Sicily or a
statue of a
smiling gallic
poet under the
towers of Avignon
something that
dreams the blue
skies of Manitoba
that imitates the
white levels the
endless defeats
of snow

Dead lakes

The dead lakes
of Sudbury
those passive
unstirring waters
without splash
without fish
without waterbugs
without breath.

The slag fires
of Sudbury
spill molten metal
on summer midnights
and the low lakes
of Sudbury
press deep into earth
under the towers
of shivering
mines.

I look down
in the dead waters
of Sudbury and
I think of Flaubert
with his crystal
Frenchness with
his one sentence
a day with his
passion for clarity
like the passion
of fish for a
living element.

And I search
for the living water
in the dead lakes
of Sudbury
and I search
for a living element
in the dead places
of my country.

Lot's wife

In your eyes
I saw suffering,
it was my own suffering.

Through your lips
I felt kisses,
they were my own kisses.

My hope reached
tall as the world,
it was your world.

The pillar broke,
light crumbled,
my heart turned
and turned to salt.

Provincial

My childhood
was full of people
with Russian accents
who came from
Humble Saskatchewan
or who lived in Regina
and sometimes
visited Winnipeg
to bring regards
from their frozen
snowqueen city.

In those days
all the streetcars
in the world slept
in the Elmwood
car-barns and the
Indian moundbuilders
were still wigwammed
across the river
with the birds
who sang in the bushes
of St Vital.

Since then I have
visited Paris
Moscow London
and Mexico City
I saw golden roofs
onion domes and the
most marvellous
canals, I saw people
sunning themselves
in Luxembourg Gardens

and on a London parkbench
I sat beside a man
who wore navy blue socks
and navy blue shoes
to match.

All kinds of miracles:
but I would not trade
any of them for the
empty spaces, the
snowblurred geography
of my childhood.

Gift: Venus 24 degrees in Virgo

For Edmund Haines

Ceremony:
a carved smiling
lazuli in a church,
brass pipes and
trumpets.

Caves, sounds,
chains, wires, loops,
saws, a ruffled
slow weave, waves

of cruel cruel
Kansas City
touching
like wheat those
tunnels, the
downrush of icy
birthwaters the
skipdip

of rolypoly
coasters, reckless
hair flying
unpaved dusty roads
the lemony glitter
in-and-out
waterfold, fishjump
the glyph, high
rush to fullfall

moontime and the
empty squares
of Madrid
filling with roses,
blowing
with white linen;

and me
saying goodbye
what gift could
anyone ever bring
you now except
to start
all over again?

New religions

I have been
converted to
all the new
religions
I agree that
the perfect
age to die
is fifty.

The perfect
control to have
is coolness and
love is the
perfect eskimo
to take to
the eternal
igloo; I have
discovered that ice
is the perfect
medium for
foretelling
the future.

There isn't
a bulb left
in the garden
there won't be
a single hyacinth
next spring
April will be
blueless.

Renunciations

1
A morning
beset with sound
salt-and-peppered
here and there
with grains of
sound

all my seeing
has disappeared
there are just
trees and

there is just
morning I open
my eyes and there
are your eyes

riddles

2
Here I am
it's morning
and your body
is sealed
anonymous as dead
snow songs

but I don't want
to hear that
music again
orphic songs are
for statues not
for living people

I want
your beard every
living hair of it
alive against
my neck why
doesn't your
body unseal
your mouth?

3
If my hands
could sing like
wheat touch
like ocean
they would
you
everywhere

Totems

I want to whittle
a new totem pole
out of a poor little
Manitoba maple and
turn all its faces
to the sun

I want to plant
it on the prairie
staring at the wind
and snow saying to
the wind: *do your
worst* and to the
snow: *mind your
mittens, don't fall
off the world naked
into the wind you
might turn to ice
or what's worse
nothingness*

I want my totem
pole to watch over
the fields against
the floods droughts and
the spoilers of space

I want the fields
and the totem pole
still to be here
when I come back a
whispering sun-ghost
or the flickering
shadow on the
hands of lovers
a thousand years
from now

Motions

You are
the lullaby
in this
arctic house
a subtle
motion from
sleep
maybe the hand
on my heart
a dark glitter
from the god
of snow

You are
the sun on glass
iridescent ships
on greenland seas
with cargo
of dancers
turning wheels
of ice

Frost breath
in my ears
long arms
of wind
wrap me in air
lift me
small person
up up
into the cradle
where I began

And you
are the lullaby.

The following

A hamper of
golden figs
was the dream-
gathering the
fiery song
of Amos;

a basket of
spoiled words
fed him in the
fountainless
desert; dazed

by ciphers
on obelisks
blanched by
centuries in
a white land
everything
passed me by;

unstrung
by silences
hungers closed
corridors
I study now
the secrecies
of Amos;

I follow
his journeys
into possible
harvestings into
ancient summers
splintered tongues;

I am preparing
to restring
the old harp
of Amos.

Tapestry

For Helen Duffy

Rags, beads, birds'
nests, straw scratchings,
summon them—the uniform
of life's fools, love's
fullnesses, dresses
for the carnivals
of custom.

Ship's lady
launcher of blue lakes
assailer of snow
shake out the quilts
of summer, scatter
my cuttings over
the ocean's propellers
and from cages of water
scoop me up, salty
newborn.

Then plant me
flower or button or
any three-pointed thing
sow me unknotted and
flowing into Mary's
wind of Easter above
her garden of ironies
fanatical, foaming
with flags.

Finding Amos in Jerusalem

He gave me
golden stones
when I wanted
stories he gave
me silence
for my blindest
furies;

He withheld
his presence he
hid his face
I hunted the
city for his
hiding place
and dug in the
rubble for his
smallest trace;

He was here he
was there he was
always nowhere
whether dragging
the weight of
a beggar's feet
or folded away
in a stranger's
frown; yet everyone
swore they had
seen him pass not
an hour before.

Above the market
or under its roofs
I listened for
the sound of those
ancient hoofs
for ghostly wheels
in the narrow streets
splashing blood of
boys with the curse
of Greece while
Egypt's hate
burned a fiery path
to Damascus Gate.

He hid from me
in an olive grove
in a cold green pit
by the Nablus road
on a January day
in the winter sun;
he called from the
bunkers he shuddered
in caves and sent out
a whisper from layers
of stone: *God is Almighty
and God is One* while the
blue song of Islam told
of brothers betrayed
then fell broken-winged
from love's scaffold.

I buried its
presence I throttled
its voice I turned
my back on the ache
of choice; my brain
was frozen my heart
was chilled my bones
were emptied and then
my eyes filled with
the seeing of Amos:
through walls of fire
and stones of gold from
the long shelves of silence
the Jewish graves rolled;
they cried against exile
two thousand years old
from the heart of grief
on a January day
on the Nablus road.

Selected Poems

Wonderful country

May was a wonderful country;
all the world's children were in pilgrimage
to greet the summer and on the way
they stopped at the zoo and lifted spells
from the golden tiger and lonely lion;
they appointed zebras their ambassadors
to laughter and they counted rabbits
surrogates of colour; on the grassy hill
they observed the peacock pondering
and down in the fen the swans
glided smooth as music and the children said:
'Let them be, they will make pillows soft as sleep,
and sleep deep as death.' So the children said
and let them be.

Around them the city flowed and the children saw
mandarin yellow leaping at them from coats
and there was chartreuse and purple—
the lanes were like a bazaar decked out
with romance for the lucky, where
across the hot-dog counter
beggars and queens came together;
oh what a clamour and shout under the palace of
    summer
as the children marched singing hallelujah to May
singing homage to May and to meadows.

Green world one

When I step out and feel the green world
its concave walls must cup my summer coming
and curving hold me
beyond all geography in a transparent place
where water images cling to the inside sphere
move and distend as rainbows in a mirror
cast out of focus.

This crystal chrysalis
shapes to green rhythms to long ocean flowings
rolls toward the sun with sure and spinning speed
and under the intensely golden point
it warms expands
until walls crack suddenly
uncup me into large and windy space.

Lullaby

Hush dove the summer
thrush lies dead deep
under withered leaves
and yellow sickled smooth.

Hush and the blue edges
of your folded wings
quiver in my hands, stain
the white apron of morning.

At dark the fluted moon
floats in the window
and the curtains weep,
their white arms

cradle your sigh and hush,
night will put a kiss
on the tired brow
of your imperilled love

and with his ribbled touch
promise you a prince,
almonds and raisins
at your feet,

rose petals and honey
against your mouth,
and on your thighs a spell
of silver needles bring.

If he never comes?
you will lie asleep
for a hundred years
on your pillared hope.

Hush uneasy grief
that curves the beetled woods,
kerchiefs folded white
between the birches blow

and night's sweet gypsy now
fiddles you to sleep
far from snows of winnipeg
and seven sister lakes.

Morning until night

1
Who could know my gothic garish life
starts so simply from morning,
when fresh and forgetful I emerge
from my red-brick tower to stride through fog?
Then I am milk-young and innocent
in the wake of alley cats,
and I am smiling and secret
against the uneasy memory of night.

The marble steps are white in the morning,
pale and white they lead to dark interiors;
I turn my eyes worshipping to the sun
see far ahead of me over the rainbow roofs
the white spear of the Italian church.

Everything praises this first moment of morning
which loops and sings into the early sky
and spreads its pure curves over the angled city.

2
At noon my light sheds its innocence and is
   absorbed
by last night's guilt, two black dogs dart out
swift as foxes to confound my eyes,
and all the sudden wolves that had my dreams
revolving on fear, startle me with their smiles;
my fears are everywhere and I through them
take changing shape.

At noon I drown, the pools of silence wash
over me in terror.

3

Gradually I enter solitude,
I open the door and where I thought to see
green meadows flowering with my name,
Miriam, written in wind, a star on the sea,
I meet only the broken face of pain
that has dogged me all day and now has found
    the way
to my secret self.   There is no place left
hidden and whole, I turn and cry
Oh God deliver me from that sad and broken face
the crippled laugh and slow relinquishing
of life, I would be transformed swift
as lightning, my evil discovered utterly
and proclaimed in its own season.

4

Two crows have I harboured long in me:
because I love doves I imprisoned crows,
forced them to silence; at night they wakened me
with constant clamour and drove sleep
beyond dawn, no one guessed the hate
feeding on silence and devouring me.

Now world mingles, feathers brush my sleep,
and doves and crows fly free.

Thou didst say me

Late as last summer
thou didst say me, love
I choose you, you, only you.
oh the delicate del-
icate serpent of your lips,
the golden lie bedazzled
me with wish and flash
of joy and I was fool.

I was fool, bemused
bedazed by summer, still
bewitched and wandering
in murmur hush in green-
ly sketched-in fields
I was, I was, so sweet
I was, so honied with
your gold of love and love
and still again more love.

Late as last autumn
thou didst say me, dear
my doxy, I choose you and
always you, thou didst pledge
me love and through the red-
plumed weeks and soberly
I danced upon your words
and garlanded these
tender dangers.

Year curves to ending now
and thou dost say me, wife
I choose another love, and oh
the delicate del-
icate serpent of your mouth
stings deep, and bitter
iron cuts and shapes
my death, I was so fool.

Unquiet world

Prophet, dream us a palm of light,
and make it bloom in our hands,
until Friday's festival
spreads its peace like wings
over the unquiet world.
Fold us smooth as shining hair
of a pious wife in slumbers sweet,
then wake us fresh with Sabbath bread
from enchanted sleep and look
with us past the templed ruins:
deep as the cratered earth
plumb our purpose, and hallowed be
the heady wine of our hope.

In the big city

On South and Fourteenth street,
wind assaulted her
dark voices shuttered her
chaos threatened her.

Then fear exploded
brilliant on trolley tracks,
a motor-cycle leaped
against a wall of flame;

a forest of faces grew
thick on the edge of night,
hot smiles crowded her,
loose elbows jostled her.

Among faces anonymous
was one she recognized,
the hunter loneliness
had stalked and followed her.

She turns now and runs
to buildings to shelter her,
her feet hold to earth,
the mother who nourished her;

Relentless the hunter
through the night follows her,
hate his ragged hound
knows love is her camouflage;

Furious they stalk the night
through the jungle streets,
terror spills its stars
over her leopard flight

And fear now feels its shape
alter with every hour;
child of itself in her,
fear is reborn

New and apart from her.
At dawn they separate
childless in empty streets
hunter covers his sightless eyes.

The music teachers

1

Was she real? Cast like a golden gargoyle
in the role of music teacher her pale hair
lit the dark winter afternoons
and her high heels sang
in sharp soprano along empty halls.
She was called Anna and her eyes
at nine were gentian but by four o'clock
the gentians closed and their blue
smudged and purled with grey.

At night she went along unlit avenues
dreaming of some lost dinner hour
to a theme of Schubert's or a serenade
by Mozart; light spilled in the street
the children whirled and in her tired mind
Scheherazade did a turn on skates,
the fabulous prince skied down the
   mountainside
dressed in white satin, his golden braid
burned her eyes until the whirling snow
filled the blank spaces.

She entered her apartment and its inky dark
curled around her, feathery plumes
licked her pale face and nested in her hair
like secrets, secrets everywhere
in all the corners and in Anna's eyes
there swam a lost Atlantis.

2

At ten o'clock, Vera, the raw-boned pianist
at the Rialto stretches; in the dressing room
her laughter is as honest as Abe Lincoln's
    gesture.
her brownswept eyes hide nothing, you can tell
she's from Missouri, a girl filled with corn
and crazy music, you can hear the pigs
capering down the mountainside in all her playing;
Vera is angled black and green and loves
to pick out noises from the piano box.
She sees beneath the lid right to its coffined heart
and she can make her audience live or die.

3

Anna (is she real?) and Vera, two music teachers,
both prisoners of winter;
Anna's gentian eyes are dying
and Vera freezes; Missouri kept her summery
for years, but this north country is hard,
nothing melts it and the scrubbled pines
crowd her memories and bleach her joy.
Anna and Vera, names of two music teachers,
with soft, foreign endings,
liquid as Noël, Ann-a, Ver-a,
and the soft soft fall
of sound on snow.

The bond

On Jarvis street the Jewish whore
smiles and stirs upon the bed,
sleep is the luxury of the poor
but sweeter sleep awaits the dead.

Sweeter sleep awaits the dead
than all the living who must rise
to join the march of hunger-fed
under the dawn of city skies.

Under the dawn of city skies
moves the sun in presaged course,
smoothing out the cunning lies
that hide the evil at the source.

I sense the evil at the source
now at this golden point of noon,
the misdirected social force
will grind me also, and too soon.

On Jarvis street the Jewish whore,
the Jewish me on Adelaide,
both of the nameless million poor
who wear no medals and no braid.

Oh woman you are kin to me,
your heart beats something like my own,
when idiot female ecstasy
transorms in love the flesh and bone;

And woman you are kin to me,
those tense moments first or last,
when men deride your ancestry;
whore, Jewess, you are twice outcast.

Whore, Jewess, I acknowledge you,
joint heirs to varied low estate,
no heroes will arise anew
avenging us twice isolate.

I who start from noonday sleep
to cry of triumph *aeroplane!*
hear nothing but the slippered creep
of famine through the surplus grain.

Exultant females shriek *parade!*
and crowd a hundred windows high,
from offices on Adelaide
they wave the khaki boys goodbye.

But heavy night is closing in,
signal omens everywhere,
you woman who have lived by sin,
and I who dwelt in office air,

Will share a common rendezvous
arranged by madness, crime, and race;
sister, my salute to you,
I will recognize your face.

Portrait

Lady by Renoir au bord de la Seine
you so synthesize Sunday
with your sun-dappled hands holding the cautious umbrella
your chameleon gown reflecting the mauve of summer
and your pointed feet
treading between hedges pruned by the gardener.

Lady by Renoir
think forward a hundred years to our Sundays
ambushed by sun no longer;
no quiet leaping between our light,
no sprigs of this or that sweetly
tickling the ankles
no river except

The slow surge of cold hatred
flowing through secret passages
under our tunnelled cities
the murder without motive
ripening in a million brains
in the dull offices
bursting like a sickness
over the angular faces of tight-lipped people
blowing an ill wind
over the sterile and severe avenues
unflanked by flowers or such frippery.

Along the close margins of the street-car tracks
cruelty travels a safe road to a smooth ending
in our familiar country.
Here kindness is pruned and love
torn up by the roots.

Sweet lady remind me of Sunday.

Does your mind
curve back to Jordan River
where the road ends and the blind
Pacific unrolls naked in sunshine?
Are your dreams
swift underwater travellers
on the ocean floor
entwined anemones and
coral branching high?

What of a smile that leaps
like a white waterfall
turning joyous cartwheels
in the sun?
And tell me if you
are coloured with the green notion
of dark-spaced orchards
clustering on the ridge
just above Shuswap
where the lake begins?

Gimli

1

I travel over you a swift railway track
spinning to Gimli's summer sudden beach:
rusty well-water, bitter, iron-tasting,
frog ditches, pockets of jelly eggs
hanging from banks;
high fenced park and between dark spruces
on the damp brown needles horny cones—
past park fence to white cottage
garden blowing with July lilies
bursting orange from nests of grass
a Polish woman, bright kerchief, keeper of two cows
rich milk foaming from leaden cans;
and the thin meadow path another year
to the house by the lake painted a chalk pink
where shrill-voiced English woman handed us
sad blue milk for our red pails.

2

So you lead to Gimli straight to
bleached sands, the gold-eye lake and
Pete the Icelandic fisherman
pushing his old boat from its moorings
paint peeling, old fish heads smelling putrid
us poking dead eyes, swinging sticky pails
later picking the sand flies from the wharf
their soft bodies crumpling in our hands
pulling at silverweed trailing its tough vines
under the poplars in stubborn network—
us sorting waterwet stones for dogshapes and spearheads
horror of sea-slime—
dragging the sand for gold, building thick ramparts.
All those castles we planted in childhood
now bear their fruit of lighted aching windows
my grief of waiting.

Summer in the street

Summer in the street was a warm welcome
drowning me in trucknoise and the shouts of children
laving me deep to my tanned arms.

Summer on the street was a sudden river
eddying me from long rain in the mountains
lifting me from introverted undertones
of the deep St Lawrence brooding in its banks
erasing the endless landscapes
of green and white silences.   Summer piloted
the sunless channels of my private mind

until I was a woman in passionate transport
of love for my own city and summer and the street;
the meadowed hush still fallow in my mind
wakened to streetcars whistling at intersections
while my eyes joyfully accepted their new focus, saw
faces of strangers each the flag of his own nation
sail past me.   Like allied ships

we read the signal of rescue and recognition
and saw the coast of our only comfort
rising from maze of streets and dead-end lanes
turned inside out, the known confusions
transformed to brilliant pointers.

Lovers

Lovers tread the waters lovers go
in all the seasons where the waters flow
they neither swim nor fly
but magically they go
where all the world envies where they go.

The world loves its lovers
and I love the waters
where the lovers go.
In spring they conquer colour
and imprison all the cries
of birds and fish within their rainbow eyes

and deep at night
you hear them wander
in the city's woods
the alleys and the streets,
you hear them cry beneath the eaves
they sigh and startle husband and his wife
from sleep, 'the lovers,' says the wife
and husband answers, 'so were we.'

The world listens and at night it hears
the silvering voice of love that pierces sleep;
all lovers weep, they neither swim nor fly
but magically they float in trees
and tread the water of the wavering will.
With all the cries of birds
imprisoned in their rainbow eyes
they go where all the world envies
where they go.

At midnight

Wife goes to husband now
and husband to his wife
the bells ring midnight on the winter
  street.

Outside the wandering cats
are still and the rooster
in his silky wing is soft asleep.

Inside the dark now
husband turns to wife
precious and single as the guarded seal

Of ancient kings
merge they and mingle,
folded limbs and lips.

Softly now falls the rhythm
of their breathing through the house
and the frost against the window flickers
  low.

Interval

Searching for the point where rivers meet
or the door that leads into a lighted room
he thought he found in woman a divining rod
that knows where all the treasure's hidden.
He thought her flesh was touched with lightning
or magic impulses that guess how rivers meet
and in her hands he saw the golden key
to vistas of unending green, blinding
the enemies of his unity.

He learned otherwise under a summer sky
embracing her one day when change of trains
left them an hour or two to kill; they fled the town
came to a field—after the rain it was—
the ground fresh and black, the last cherries
withering on bushes, and dried raspberries
clinging to fences, a sleepy cow in pasture
the distant rumble of freight cars
heading for city.

They lay down together and they kissed,
and in that kiss he felt his past defeats
narrow and bind him and his dream grown large
filled the light sky to its cloudiest limits
stretched like a bubble and as quickly broke.
The dream fell and gave him back
himself in a thousand pieces
all separate and disjointed.
Then he knew there is no golden key
no one has hidden it, there is no joyous room
where man completes his marriage in a moment,
there are no easy signposts, only a lonely road
that each one travels with his suffering.

Catalpa tree

Catalpa, in you a song, a cache
a secret story hidden
a cat, an alp to climb, an ahhh—
winedrinker's joy and almost the apache
of violent lunges, whisperings backstage.
And still the greenery, the lacings of the leaves
with quiet, wind outside
and inside cool, cool as caves
or water, cool as waves
and welcome as water is
on salted skin and ankle.

Here is everness,
and gliding of the light
into some brilliant world where it enjoys
its own infinity, here I taste the grass
and touch the springy blossoms dry as silk,
think such was I and such my child may be
if grace grows leaves and listening multiplies
and trees yield up their wordless therapy.

In the sun

The world was not more or less
because we looked at it, or so
our reason told us; but our eyes
told us more truly otherwise; we were blind.
A sea of grass pounded in our ears, a wind
of branches brushed us, we were dumb;
we stood and listened, the gritty meadow sang.

Was it the sun's fullness
or the apple tree's eclipse, or were we
really new?   The thorn of the barbed wire fence
pricked us, and we stood exactly the same height,
brown eyes to blue, and nothing moved
except the yellow colour of my dress
and your shirt of white.

I said, 'It smells of strawberries here,'
and bent down to look.   'Don't pick them now.'
It was you who spoke, you who moved your arm
with its million fine gold hairs and shut out
the strawberry plants, their literal green
and the way they grew in the rough crab grass
with the wet spit of the spider's dew; it was you.

I stood up and in the sun I looked at you;
we judged each other, man and woman.
And the sluggish river lay beyond the field
where the invisible insects hummed,
and from the clump of trees the sightless song
of birds plummeted; almost it seemed
these voices were our children calling us.

You were the man, I took your arm, and over us
the sun full shone; in me the world was more.

In the park

The child follows the sun
dizzy, lost in the circling asters
and the criss-cross of dripping
delicious honeysuckle
all the pink and exploding delicacy.
Oh what a curtain it makes for the myth
the haunted oedipus, a modern backdrop
  a very
innocence of plants and children!

And mothers, indirect, elliptical
under their shady hats
nod at sailboats while their smiles
pull in stormy adventurers
and their gestures
make such graceful patterns
willy nilly on the sun dial.

But I like some great eclipse
cut off the starry light
and teach him afternoon as if it were
religion, I'm a familiar island
hard and rock-bitten, though where
the footprint leads he cannot guess.
Unanonymous I sit, the green park benches
make me a giant, and of course
my glance is threatening.

Night in October

(The dream, the dream, where did it begin?
In the downpour of light that flooded through the sky?
Where was the key that opened up the door
to a white room with candles burning?)

At midnight the wind
stretched long leathery fingers
against the warm night
lifted the roof of torment and sang
lullabies from an old book
of apples and nutmegs and peacocks that flew
ceaselessly circling a golden sea.
(It was dream, it was dream,
light echoes and keys were lost in the sea.)

Then pain came with its symphony
with its many players
who tuned forceps and scissors
and the sharp cruel dancers
who whirled and galloped
all over my girlhood, shipwrecked and bitter.
(There was an answer, I heard it through water
through the coils and columns
but it was lost in the weather
the genesis of snow.)

The dream the dream
that nested like a dove
in evergreens and eaves,
that fed on angel honey
and loaves of silky bread
the dream still nameless
wandering and restless
searching for me.

I in my torment was chained to the moment
heard the harsh rasp of wire
and the ring of steel
on vast white porcelain—
all over the prairie my prayers were empty
all over the ocean my hands had spread
and the doctors were dancing

Fandangoes boleros
they sang commands in a chorus
of feverish laughter *once more and again*
and now die again, yes die, yes die
so I died just to please them.

(But the dream, the dream, where did it begin?
In jewels, in stars, in powdery snow
Or sin? Oh lullabies be quiet and still
the dandelions do die and on my graveyard green
their white petticoats of lace upon the hilltop blow
and pebbles bleached and dry
neatly line the path.)

From far away a voice
calls me from the dead:
are you there are you there
are you there? Urgently jolted
out of death without warning
I wake to the new child's crying—
it is morning morning
full of problems and sorrow.

(Light fades from the window
and the dream nameless and wandering
goes to sleep in its echoes
unsolved and insoluble.)

Inward look the trees

How inward look the trees;
loverlike they stretch
needful they beseech
mercy from the skies
they pour into my eyes
a largeness full of light
they lift their crowd of leaves
and urge me to believe.

Their silence seems to slight
the threat that's in the air,
the storms here and there,
the furious hurricane and
the schizophrenic plane.
Oh danger danger pass
over this square of grass
and take no note of me
under this vase of tree.

If the poisonous splash
of an atom's broken breath
or the touch of a cruel
splitting molecule
withers, burns, destroys
when inward look the trees
and upward takes my eye
to see how high they fly
the birds, in glossy joy—
on that day, my death,
pass me by, pass me by.

Seashell

When a shell forsaken
by its creature lies
the good of shellness
goes, instead it holds
its shape as memorized;
frail and bleached
it curls like breath
(or death)
against the arm of beach.

Or else brought here it lies
dry and intricate
upon my desk
(remembering the sea
or winking with irony
at my child and me?)

Laughter

We are light
as dandelion
parachutes we
land anywhere
take the shape
of wherever we
fall

we are often
the size of
grasshoppers in
a jungle of grass
or we're squirmy
chains of willow
catkins

then we become
curly seashells
knobby little
swimmers in a
sea of air
lying

on our backs
our eyes fly up
higher than kites
airplanes clouds
winds higher
than stars

we stare down
at the little
distant world
and we laugh
laugh laugh

City street

Walk there when it's quiet
and the people are asleep,
along the white aisles of spirea
churching the darkness, move.
You can hear the hot night buzz
through the thin whirr and warm crackle
of crickets under leaves.
You can smell the small sweet buns
of honeysuckle and in your mind's eye see
the burning day that wore upon its breast
flaming Japonica, coloured in high key,
and sweet
sweet as the song about Venezuela.

The hockey players

Stiff as flowers
lined up beside park benches
the child hockey-players
parade their colours;
under the heavy helmets
their eyes weave a garland
of constant wonder.

Who has planted them
in the forest of winter
so far from their childhood?
Who are those giant spectators
who chopped down the summer
and now fill the arena
with loud expectation?

Investigator

I who am street-known am also street knowing:
just ask me—
I know the tangle of hot streets behind the poorhouse
pouring from the city like coiled intestines,
the smell of the brewery as it splays long fumes
in the alleys
and the streets pushed against the zoo
with litter of peanut shells and empty candy boxes;
also the streets climbing crazily up the river bank
between bridge and jail.

My hand knows the familiar gesture
of measuring a child's height in passing;
even if I were blind I would see the grey figure
hear the thin high call of the city's authorized
salvage collector.
I could tell you, and no exaggeration,
of the in and out of houses twenty times a day
of the lace antimacassars, the pictures of kings and queens
the pious mottoes, the printed blessings, the dust piling
up on bureaus,
the velour interiors, the Niagara souvenirs
the faded needlepoint, the hair pulled tight
and the blinds drawn against day and the feel of sun.

Then down between lake and railway tracks
the old houses running to seed, the grass grown tall
the once-mansion made into quaint apartments
where a foul granny with warts all over her face
sits counting last year's newspapers lost in a timeless litter
and her hunchback son runs nimble messages with covetous eyes.

Out on the street again into the fainting heat
where bloom the rank garbage cans to the jazz of trolleys,
past the garden where the old man drooling senile decay
lets the sun slip ceaselessly through his fingers,
and for humour
a long lean lap-eared dog sitting on a roof
blinks wet eyes at me.

Getting older

So suddenly I shed
the dull, the brown, the faded winterberry
and become the red
passionate dictionary
full of scattered words and wider meanings,
hidden synonyms,
a world of undone acts, of tremblings, leanings
and unassembled limbs.

Something like old times
I sense the bulb, the hidden impulse stir,
I feel the rhymes
though wobbly and unsure
plain and homely, creep into the place
marked *private no trespassing here*
where lies a field, a little sparrow space
that is inside and near.

Sympathy

'I could have been in California
over a rolling road of bootlegged rum barrels,
but they fooled me—
I'm handsome but I'm not lucky.'
Sit down and tell me your full dream
of dry goods store and your own children,
and I will answer with the round technique
that walls me from you;
give your misfortunes, I'll remember mine.

Mister I could have been in California
if the perfect football had rolled in a perfect field
if I had not been blanketed in bleachers
or listened to the whispers from the loges—
man, I could have stridden this world
any autumn day or moved the pillars
that held up the sky. I could have then.

The zig-zag laughter that zoomed horizons crashed;
hallos were stifled in areaways and somehow
the silk threads of love were tangled.
I'm not lucky either—
so tell me your misfortunes, lay your plans,
I'm listening with one ear to my past.

Folkways

To conductors on streetcars mumbling
'move along there, move along,'
I would answer, 'what's your hurry brother?'
slowly and maybe smile.

To slums in odd corners of cities
hidden behind smoke-stacks
waiting for me to discover their sorrows
(come today, lady from welfare, come today)

I would go straight as the crow flies,
arrowing over the Don and its leafy mudlands,
over the brickyards, over the scooped ravines,
the most direct route.

Travelling on crowded streetcars,
swerving round corners called Castlefrank
I am confused by advertisements
engrossed by the hurrying faces.

So do not wonder when I knock at battered doors
if my smile is cold, drawn tight over afterthoughts.

House of industry

Sorrow is not a kind sister
Trailing dispensation in her wide sleeves
sorrow is not benign
bears no blessings.

Sorrow is the strict almshouse where
comfort is doled by government regulation,
excluded are those idle, dissolute and undeserving
who throw themselves upon the public bounty,
only the pious adepts, practised at talking poormouth
are granted the foursquare peace, the limited bed
the secret locker.

Here temporary outcasts come to sit
in the narrow courtyard set aside for them
waiting for the sound that sends release
echoing from wall to whitewashed wall
as they hear the trusty calling out a name.

Sorrow is not a kind sister.

Toronto
the golden-vaulted city

I'm in a rich cold city,
Toronto the golden-vaulted,
runnelled and hollowed,
British born, steeped by cliffs,
axed by watercourses,

its warehouses pure Ontario,
its lake like Michigan,
and all its warm bungalows
lighted with midwinter's
scarcity of snow.

Alas poor York;
the howling wind outside
shakes the grey plateau,
stalks the gothic arches
in the dark moist marketplace,
follows under the overpass,
pursues like Caligari
in subway alleys
where the white-tiled breath
of unearthly cold
foretastes the sooty grave.

Dragon-tall is my adversary;
from arctic cold he rises,
but I am murdered, bloodless
in the untenanted subdivision
among the broken bricks
and chickenwire debris
I'm dry as last year's berries
under the frozen hedge.

The moundbuilders are dead
in my native province,
the grain elevators
are locked on the lakehead,
and the vaulted city blazes
like a many-pronged golden
pitchfork stabbing the clouds
for light.

Journey to the clinic

1
Into the white hush of quiet suburb
crisp with fading winter, crackle of a tree
and eight o'clock sunshine
morning precedes me.
Past the bay and bark of dog
licked, possessed, identified
by the curiosity and knowledge of my street—
my footsteps lead me.
Through the sugary snow I splash
on to the terminus where light gleams
palely, weighted by the buzz
and bell of trams, the grind of wheels
the deep unease of crowds.
Something in me cries
'Go back!' I hesitate,
ahead of me the journey warns:
this morning is too late.
Then all hurry to move towards,
we dark the waves, are flailed through the doors.

2
Oh lovely ocean!
We sway like mermaids on these leather straps
and dream of seaweed.
Above us trains explode
to giant anemones and though we root for light
are dizzy, drink the neon signs,
we are denied
our thirst is multiplied.
Below us the crane quarries the city
and steam shovel spreads a naked garish claw.

3

Watch these indifferent builders dredge
the soul of my city, see how they gauge decay
to unthought levels and how they spit up sand
with melting snow and all the steaming stench
of gaping sewers; there is no mercy here
for ripped-up road-beds, skeleton pipes
or the delicate fins of danger;
filled with machinely humour
they wink their monstrous eyes and lift their arms
to bar all entry and point a detour—
where?

4

All sailors rally!
There is no out, no under or above;
we're on a narrow course, bound
to the canals and rivers of the city
the chasms, tenements and yellow meeting halls.
Anonymous we swim these deeps
these whales of misery
and through the glass
drink bitter orphanage.
On tides of noise the little children rise
from playground to day nursery
(through the miles of space
I hear a sandpiper sing).

5

Then clarion comes the call
The cry bilingual
Guy-Gee, Guy-Gee—it is my sesame.

I make the steep descent
On to cement and kerb
Down to the sluggish grey
of Saint Antoine's shore-line:
farewell my ship and sky
farewell my mates
who rocketing go on
to the fair city.

6

Here is my inner world;
it has a thousand smells,
all welcome me, the smell of soup
of children's feet and pee.
Little children, fishes in the net
Of doctors, dentists and their instruments
you are the captives here;
locked inside a sleep
of counted minutes you will wake
to morning filled with fluttering cries
missing a tooth or curiously
gazing at bandaged arm or thigh
(is this the place, the station of your dream?)

7

This is no harbour;
it is instead the place
where years of make-do
months of minimums
and all the world of poor
at last have brought you.

Call up the demons
let them scale the tree
that waves its flag
and flickers green to me
in my most inward glimpses
and pray they'll meet
good fairy True-Heart
whose sweet skill can ring
these walls with health
like some gold glowing rope.

May her wand transform
the evil of disease
and to all stricken bones
bring bandages of light;
beseech her clever touch
(and more, her loving brain)
against your clouded dreams
of injury and wreck.

Will we defeat the death
that waits within these walls
(and in the world outside)?
And will we from the rain
the soot the hundred-years-old stains
from tired travelling
find our sleep unhaunted
and get the strength to build
palaces whose walls
stay white against the rain
marbled and mild?

The thief

Armand Perrault, petty thief
what do I know of your belief?
I have seen the brown-robed monks in spring
with sandalled feet go clattering
down the hill on Côte des Neiges
your church with golden roof a cage
for wandering birds and captive saints.

I have watched your little sisters go
solemn to their first Communion
with veils askew and hair ablow—
stiff paper bouquets in their hands
and flimsy crosses on their necks,
then seen them hide by the stone cliff
of some poor church in Maisonneuve.

From the same parish, aunts in hats
green and painted loud as parrots
have issued forth to board the buses;
between their words, small cries, and fusses
I've heard their false teeth click and clamour
and answered with my English stammer.

However I try to imagine you
Armand Perrault, you don't come through.
At nine years old on a clinic bench
in shorts cut down from your father's pants
with braces too wide for your narrow
    shoulders
or leaning against your mother in church,
you heard the priest at his masses and
    mutters;
Or I see you beside the kitchen stove
nursing a toothache with camphor and clove.

Let's try the path your memory takes,
follow the thread until it breaks:
it was hot, from the oak buffet you took
your mother's purse though fingers shook;
you longed for money, the weighty coins
that fell in the pool of your future years
with widening circles; thread breaks here—
the first time you stole, however clear
you figured the reason in later years.

Reasons have not much place with us;
I listen astonished to what you say
about honour and friends and the clever way
there is to stealing and then you ask
disregarding this room, this desk—
if I wouldn't do the same as you
if you were me and I were you?

This is the point we spin around
and this is the answer I haven't found
what have I learned from talking to you
apart from the tricks every pickpocket knew
before he left the public school?
Apart from the pride that is the rule
among the friends you tell me of,
your story is familiar enough.

I haven't heard much that was new to me
or brought any word that was new to you;
it seems our separate selves must curve
wide from the central pulsing nerve
which ought to unite us, you and me;
and only our social selves can meet,
like foreign sympathies, touch and greet,

And out of this force, this difference, build
a small safe area; a bridge; a shield.

The women's jail

This garden is outlandish
with its white picket fence
and straggling orchard;
who would guess this painted house
with convent walks
is a women's jail?

Unless you had seen their faces,
old women grey as sponges
drooping in this habitat
young ones sullen
with a worm gnawing them.
I often wonder why the drug-takers
have such skyblue eyes.

And the cheque-forgers:
how velvet they are
how apples and cream,
secretly I envy them
their blossoming bodies
and their talents with men.

Being especially human
I am no judge of evil
but hear how it has
a singing life in them
how it speaks out
with an endowed voice.

Doubt my poor, my gentle one
my overtrained, my fine
my inner ear.

I have been insufficiently dowered
my limbs are pale as winter
sun-starved
my blood is free from alcohol
I am law-abiding, I am completely
resistible—is there anything
praiseworthy in that?

Old women of Toronto

All old women sometimes come to this:
they go to live away, they cross ravines,
mornings they ride the subway, later look below
to read the red of dogwood and the print of snow.
They tread upon the contours of each month
with delicate feet that hardly sense its shape,
explore the mouth of March and with a hiss,
they spit at myth and swallow counter-bliss.

Their brows beetle, their plush hats tremble
they specially deplore without preamble
the palomino carpets on the lawns
steamy with manure in frosty air;
against all evidence and witnesses they'll swear
they never argued once or schemed to take
the room in front with the old Morris chair,
and partial view, at least, of the bright lake.

Two prison portraits

1. THE ALCOHOLIC

Ericson, this time you came sober
eyes unclouded by your dream of heaven;
humble again, the wild visioning over
you came to say that you were dough to leaven.
Your eyes still bloodshot sent out a tremor
shaking you like leaves and pulse's hammer
tapped through your muscles merciless;
again I had to write *No fixed address*
and smell you, not quite animal or medicinal
but harsh and winey, stale, of alcohol.

Bitter you glinted and cold Norway blue
kindled through frosty loneliness—
did you melt for a moment or raise your pride
to its old equal? Your hands hung shrunken white
from lack of work but something lighted you;
Ericson, don't ask me how, but once for all
will you cut fjord, unleash lakes, and swim?

2. THE DRUG ADDICT

Kingly were his rags, his uniform
was tatters and fair his unshaven face;
his eyes were lighted as if some other world
informed them of perfection closed to us.

What other world could turn his twenty years
from orphanage and factory nurtured by
    machines
to such a bright disorder, what genius could
    abash
his heaven-inspired eyes ablaze with heroin?

His glory tumbled later, tumbled with the hair
moist as cornsilk and flushed against his skin;
age could not tutor him nor gods confine
him to our places—his will outshone

His chances, its brilliance bruised our eyes;
he went down like a hero defending his own
    kind
and in some paradise which still eludes our
    lust
he climbs the beanstalk and with a shadowy
    knife

Stabs at the giant, cuts the glittering dust
and cries at the blood of his own life.

My lessons in the jail

Walk into the prison, that domed citadel
that yellow skull of stone and sutured steel,
walk under their mottoes, show your pass,
salute their Christ to whom you cannot kneel.

In the white-tiled room arrange the interview
with the man who took his daughter and learn
that every man is usual but none are equal
in the dark rivers that in them burn.

And take this man's longest bleakest year
between done act and again-done act, and take
his misery and need, stand against his tears
and transform them to such a truth as slakes

The very core of thirst and be sure
the thirst is his and not your own deep need
to spurt fine fountains; accept accept
his halting words—since you must learn to read

Between the lines his suffering and doubt.
Be faithful to your pity, be careworn,
though all this buffet you and beat and cruelly
test you—you chose this crown of thorns.

Wear it with grace and when you rise to go
thank him and don't let yourself forget
how hard it is to thank and to beholden be
one to another and spin your role out yet

For moments in the hallway, compose your face
to false good humour, conceal your sex:
smile at the brute who runs the place
and memorize the banner *Christus Rex.*

Christ in a loin cloth

Christ in a loin cloth
Tarzan in another
how am I to know
which is my brother?

Swinging from a tree
or nailed to the cross
which is really free
or pleads a higher cause?

Prison be to me
as forest is to one
and prison build for me
a scaffold to the sun.

Make my thirst as clear
as of an animal and
make my hunger sharp
to bite through my skull.

Invent with me a plan
to undo the cross
to pluck out the thorns
or cushion them with moss.

And like a tree revealed
lift your face to light
man may still be free
and wrong defend the right.

Stand divine and green
immutable and staunch
redeem the dove redeem
from death and broken branch.

Trip from the city

When I made my trip from the city
there were doors I passed
some were painted red
some were painted green
and from the streetcar I could see
the snow had fallen white.

And later the freightyards;
skimming the swamp, the brown miles
of tundra, we rocked past all
the black skeletons of trains
marooned in the world
we flew through the tundra
of dead lines and unhumming machinery.

How was I to believe the river
after the tunnel
when it suddenly happened?
The river making a darkened gash
heavy and frowning,
leaning into the pale snow.

It happened, right in my eyes
a miracle flooded, growing water
closed them and billowed them
far far from the terrible confusion
of wounding tracks and the remorseless level
of the yards, the land of poor
and all unlighted trains.

Charity

Down down into the namelessness
the streets like sooty wells
that drown you in their pools
of brackish torpor and struggling hold you
unwilling as you are.

Down down to the faces bleached
and leaning as the line of houses,
to where the street pursues
the fathers as they search
darkness flaring with the high
brief alcoholic joy; the mothers wait
and in the half-lit rooms
their hands are exposed and eager.
There you will find the door
and all you know waits there
so enter.

Enter and like a swimmer plunge
still deeper into darkness;
breathe their damp despair and mouth
the bitterness of begging, spit it like a coin
for luck, at least you found it once.
Maybe this small gleam
will travel through the ocean's high blind miles
to strike a younger eye, a greener hope
and fields of meditation find.

Pleasures from children

Er ist gewesen, I tell you,
absolutely on top of the world,
then he went whoring and
she got him, the little snake.
Das ist ein Maedchen?
He will pet her and pet her
until she will curl around him,
then she will hiss out
and bite him the poisonous
thing; she got him
and he was a king I tell you
the gold poured through his hands
and I carried him on my shoulders,
was there anything too good?

I know I know,
I know what she intends
with her low love tricks;
a boy needs to go to a woman
now and then, but to that slut
that serpent? Oh why don't you
see that my father's heart
is in sackcloth, why don't you
absolutely from the top of the world
help me?

Sea bells

Five fathoms deep my father lies
and of his bones are my bones made
this is his blindness in my eyes
his limping paced my grave.

Oh daughter toll the sea-green bell
and shake the coral from your hair
the sea was once your bed of birth
your given name your knell.

My body was your sepulchre
the wide world was your cell
my hand has written in your blood
what time and tide will tell.

The tide has since cast up its scroll
and told what time could tell;
five fathoms deep my father lies
his daughter deeper fell

To see the seeing of his eyes
and take what pearls might have to give;
five fathoms deep in sleep he lies
whose death waked me to live.

Saint Antoine Street

1
(HURRY)
The hungry word
uncurls like a fern
in the odd silence
falling at noon

the street is like a forest
of white trees and negro underbrush
full of furious growing;
the pavement spills
its nameless colour;
I wade ankle deep in it
lost and puzzled.

Nervous with the noise of trains
the crash of stop, the gust of go
I circle rising storms of soot;
the quiet language of slow
gets lost, and awkward
as a grounded bird
I blink my eyes while in my brain
jumps the hungry laggard word
(HURRY)

2
The pale shiver of leaves
against soot and brick
is like the white astonishment
of shells all curled
and tasting like surprise
of chalk and briney;

or it feels like a gentle wave
that greeningly assaults
our city eyes and leaves them
somewhat wounded, filled
with lack of love;

these shimmering crazy trees
just halfway alive, just gentle
being trees
become a mathematic and disclose
philosophy, argue with hunger,
haggardness and perspiring hours.

With their gentle stirrings
they ignore the soot;
sun makes them beautiful
and they brush the sky
with secret fullness.

Dark and shining
they reproach our dearth.

Night on skid row

My blood shudders but I dream
of a bad country overcome,
of torn flags and murmuring
in burnt-out cities; what is as cold
as the anticlimax of return,
the soldier with his missing limb?
There aren't a dozen burning words
to give or take or smoke in chains,
and hardly a curse to knock about
in the fogged arena of the brain.

The clever thief of forty-odd
wakes sober in the boiler room,
he feels his cancer sharp as God,
but doesn't think this is the time
to pen a *billet-doux* to Christ
(the lying poet's bleeding heart);
instead, he knots his shirt and goes
across the valley's bridge to find
the village where his father died.

And the Irish pickpocket
alias barker-out-of-work
resumes his habit *ave, evoe,*
the heroin is organized
with rich disaster in his veins;
stork-like he reels and teeters
and blind with love he dreams
he's king of the rainbow carnival
and the city is his vassal.

Doris with her crooked bones
locked in a child's haunted world
is glad to be the scissor's wife,
to trim the thread from uniforms.
Her friend, a hotel chambermaid,
from eight to six on Sherbrooke-*strasse*
stumps the unemployment clerk
who reads her face and shakes his head:
she'll never shape into the work.

I met them all in their defeat;
their words, of narrow local colour,
fell in wider provinces
than their travels would allow.
A crowd of accents was dispersed
through all the shabby streets I know,
where night, erect with violence,
disgorged police from limousines;
I heard the whistle on the air
and hung, and splintered from the blow.

Poets and statues

She treads delicate as love on Craig Street
and picks her way among the pawnshops' signs
she drowns in heat, drinks steam for a libation
and has nothing to pawn except a public word.

And nothing to buy that's personal to her
neither necklace nor ornament, it is long since
beauty explained her or a man's hand traced
the song of Solomon against her breast.

Her Solomon is nowhere: Sheba-less
he speaks the verse of everyman to brick and stair
he stands in the hot square of the midcity
and his praise is not her dark her midnight hair

or her belly's wheat or oiled skin or myrrh.
His lovesong is the derelict's cold awaking
the dying woman's cry against her death
the drunkard's protest that he has no children;

it is the servant girl's lock and key of riches
the however touch of fatherly seducer
the bachelor dreaming through the double feature
and the Indian riding on a bus all night
returning with a sick and coughing fortune.

Who can say this queen is passionless
or if she hears the city's desperate love?
Maybe within the desert reaches of her ear
a watergush still waits to irrigate
the silence where there sleeps a buried song;

at evening she walks in aimless blindness
into the small green park where four walls meet;
she stops before a statue painted gold
and touches the mute face; the wooden forehead
lives beneath her fingers, the eyebrow is rough.
The wood is cold yet she is not amazed
to feel her hand wet and scalded by its tears.

The mile runner

You are my buzz my hive, you are my honey steeple,
you are my me my how my pray and also prithee
my mile runner and spinning helicopter
my rescue from the wilderness of river.

And are you not my this my that of prairie
my weathered granary, my nuisance crow?
My miles of sameness and my endless railway,
my gone-astray, my slow unlabelled freight?

So add the fishes' double-quick of colour
the while-away of summer's brazen boys
the golden eye of lakes, the fresh of beaches
and I'm the eyelid and the tongue and I'm the ear.

The city's life

She is a woman possessed by cities
in love with imperfect faltering man,
her time is taken with analysis
of eyes screened off by glasses, thinning hair
blood out of season, limbs that scan
with perfect measure to the count of death:
these elements freeze into the air
or melt against the salt of road beneath,
and bring her to a strange inverted bliss.

She has no face to fit such ancient pities;
she knows of old the loose-limbed syphilitic
who shuffles beneath the city's towered clocks;
the unshipped seaman who has no union card
is as familiar as her own sharp headache—
the thief, impelled by frequent search for mother
reads life as she does, mean and hard;
lonely; no sister swallow, no bird-brother
listens to their songs or inner talks.

She does not own the burglar's forcing tools
or have his abstract grasp of puzzling parts;
all she has are her own human channels
eyes that observe, a pulse that beats
a heart that moves to other troubled hearts;
somewhere she keeps her mind's prepared collation—
projects, theories, and some orphan facts;
but she is impatient and values them much less
than all the discontinuous evidence
which haunts her every step and holds her powerless
against the city's life, its crowded annals.

Things of the world

A north Winnipeg girl
bending over water
she spent her summers at a lake
and watched the goldeye swim.

Later in the neon season
of an eastern city
she ate its white flesh
off the spiced rainbow skin.

The good things of the world
she learned long ago
from the sun out there
in the prairies, in that light

caught frogs and birds
picked hazelnuts and found
lady's slipper in a leafy ditch,
skull-and-cross-boned trees.

She played with Indian children
across the river in the saint
settlements and was converted
by the golden statues

to a blazing innocence
easy to learn, but the other
things that harmed her
(even herself), those
she could never explain.

The field of night

For Philip Surrey

Messiah will not come
and I must sing the time
that every poet knows
so ravel up the threads
the golden fleece of song,
seize armfuls of cloud
above the gilded domes
of Moscow's onion roofs
and spin the world round.

And I will read the time
from sundials in the air
where London used to sleep
and Paris frivolous
danced on teetering feet;
the hives of all New York
swarmed in the trees
and neighbours did not keep
to caves and private work.

Our cowardice is known
and all the ill is done,
alone or with another
the body is our brother;
and Messiah will not come
though we may wait the time
till kings of good become
the presidents of wrong,
there's nothing left but time.

Such time as others shape
to their elected hopes
with songs that rise above
the golden concert halls
or reach of telescopes;
there my defeated choirs
sing in broken keys
of all the doors I forced
by solar acts of love.

The wind has howled them shut
and sealed them in my blood;
and all the frozen songs
that winter in the north
lie on a field of night
they wait the touch of sun
and I am sick and dumb;
the fastness of the world;
Messiah, when will you come?

The gardeners

Last spring I wished
for myself a fullgrown garden;
night and day in my mind's eye
summer turned out its pockets
for me, spilled flowers and birds,
impaled the four winds in fossils.
I dreamed of rare specimens
and ordered forsythia lilac
and flowering almond bushes.

Strong with hope I began to dig
but the clay would not move
under my hand or foot or shovel;
I hacked away in my backlot
to the heart of North America
(virgin stone dammit) until my hands
trembled with failure; then I cried
as bitterly as a nine-year-old.

And later wondered is this
my father's daughter, this
rag-petalled wind-blown tear-
stained love-me love-me-not daisy?
This everything-ventured-nothing-gained
sorrykins, this no-more-young ineptitude?
This is not me or she my father's
daughter; it is some drag and hag
throwback to Abishag the devil took
and take hellish mistake!

And my father? For him
whole fields of cucumber
ripened by the riverside and
the small-leaved orchards grew.
Nowhere inherited I am
his redhaired melancholy
ten generations deep and steep
his course historical nourished
with skill, a proud harvest
heaped and reaped for ruin.

Yet he my father when aged sixty-eight
was bleached and humming as a field of wheat
grew a grapevine in a city lot
with stems thick as your arm,
had flowers rioting, incited evergreens
and against all nature harvested
in Toronto an Arizona melon.

Fortunes

There is something in all of us
pure and unconsumable;
after the forest fires
on the logged-over hillsides
you find the stubborn flowering
of fireweed or a green tree
hung with a grab-bag of prophecies:
you will live long you will go on ocean voyages
you will be lucky in love or unlucky
beware the queen of spades a handsome stranger
will come into your life—the choices
are dazzling.

But whatever you do
it will end the same;
we are not all lucky and the stranger came
but stayed a stranger; we lived
unhappily ever after and the queen of spades
dug my grave; after the ten-thousandth evening
of dumb show and furious pantomime
fed up with Punch and Judy
I went out into the autumn night
to cry my anger to the stone-blind fields
just as I was, untraditional, North American
Jewish, Russian, and rootless in all four,
religious, unaffiliated, and held
in a larger-than-life seize of hate.

It was then I felt my own purity:
I felt the young girl in me
still like a green tree growing
tall and rooted, with a promise of flowering,
whatever bastardy flower I could flower with now,
a *shloime-kapoir* Solomon-upside-down flower;
and why not? I always think of the Russian word
for soul, *dusha,* and the dusty Slavic village
smelling so sweet with the grass uncut
and the white lilacs blooming, like a homecoming
for my homeless half-and-half soul.

And I felt a kind of raised eyebrow
yes-this-is-me, this is no-one-else
not the laidly worm of Spindlestone
no longer the bewitched princess,
but a wonderful living statue of marble stone
with her garments sculptured,
sailing against the wind of death.

Three poems for my teacher

1
I wish your death be magic as your life
as loved and loving and as full
as seeded summer in its flurried colour.
I wish you quiet hush and holy
as this morning and I wish
all voices lost and gone
and all those voices mourning
return to attend your ending.
You are a fortunate mother to be so loved
by all your children, our words and thoughts
transform you and we keep
in this mortal world your spirit
young forever and your name
by our humanity is hallowed.

2
Now with the warm surge of summer
your spirit haunts me and the lawns
of this foreign city speak
your benediction, your white touch
stirs the long still avenues
where married couples walk in double silence.
It is your hand which steadily retrieves
their glances from the whirlpools
and your voice the flow of sound
which oboes through the melancholy
tangles of the soul;
strong as sunlight every day
you burn your place in time

and timeless, drowned in love, my dream
sinks deeper in the layers of the city,
becomes a pale figure and revolves
gently on the swell of traffic.
There is an ultimate moment far from now
and it will fall without warning
at the instant of death;
in the street no passerby will mark
your portrait in the galleries of water
and your face still smiling.

3
Beyond the white gothic of her smile
far pools of stillness lie
and the summer wind
plays the green mandolins of her voice
her words are plain as ballads and they sing
the flowering season and the moving space
between waking and sleeping
and then the final sleep.

Poem for a pupil

Imprisoned in the pillar of your throat
I am the word, the phrase, the sentence you create
I am your best, your self, your beautiful
or maybe your disease.

In the valleys of your arms
I am the slumbering wish that stills
the springs and rivers and at last awakes
the rushing torrents.

In your sleep I am that crucial dream
whose meaning you forget, whose imprint paints
a restless landscape you cannot locate
in waking moments.

And in the pageant of your blood
I am incessant war, the foreign knight who sees
your flowering cells both red and white
turn cannibal and devour.

Helpless in this prison I have shaped
myself to you, inside your brain and bone
where I will be your health, your joy
or maybe your disease.

Exchange

When brandy burns in the air
and forests hold their winter sleep,
when Byron dark and Shelley fair
their appointed places keep;

when rhyme and reason fancy free
join inside my heart and head,
when you become the voice of me,
and I the rib of all you said;

then will the core of this exchange
fall and grow into a tree
with leaves embroidered rare and strange
with gloss of you and text of me.

From a dead poet's book

There was the sound
of your breathing
and your voice
saying *forever*
a word from a line
in a dead poet's book.

There was light
from a candle
there was a wall
and a forest and
darkness an island
with yourself

and myself floating
from sleep we
watched last autumn's
love apples fanning
and tossing on seas
in the darkness

and through darkness
and light felt
snow on the rooftops
in a distant city in
a lonely nightwatch;
there was the sound

of your breathing,
like a burning garland
forever hung above us,
winter burned, apples
glittered and words
froze on the branches;

and everywhere in
darkness was *forever*
and everywhere in
darkness was your
voice and everywhere
the distant city and
everywhere (I almost
said) everywhere was
my love

The snows of William Blake

Grant me such snows that I may bear
Iberian night without complaint,
and pastures for my green despair
if summer still remains.

Grant me arrows of desire
shaped from boughs of burning gold
and wound me with their constant fire
until my life grows old.

Then grant me skulls and skeletons
for the wind to whistle through
and may the singing of my bones
never ring untrue.

If my spirit still should yearn
for one whose absence I forgave
raise a golden bough to burn
above my lighted grave.

Children's coloured flags

Do you remember the house
where my mother died, it was
winter and the quince trees
slept outside the window
on the day you first kissed me
it seemed as if life itself
was scribbling gay messages
all over children's coloured flags.

Do you remember how we talked
about *jamais je ne t'oublierai*
and about the snow piling up
in the cities we had slipped
out of and about all those lives
that had melted away, but who
can say how it really was?

Since that day death and
other winters fell upon
the house; the trees were
cut down the florist's car-
nations died in the flower-
water of the vase, people
died, I made many poems
and the house still stands

shabby and white; the grass
has long ago covered the
place where quinces grew; life
still scribbles its messages
and how blind I was not to
see in the random waving
of children's coloured flags
the declaration of war.

You are my never

You are my never and I your no one am
this is the sum and score of all our bliss
nothing is our warmest deepest touch,
and distance, our cold and laving kiss.

Since I am no one and you never are
we find our footing in the worlds we spin
and though we're polar and must lie apart
we have our tropic where we fuse within.

We cross no fields no cities and no miles
for nothing needs no medium to sin
here never loves his no one with denials
and arbitrates against himself to win.

So be my never and long may nothing live,
bless all distance and intensity
which strain our kisses through a starry sieve
and drowning you have also here drowned me.

The land
where he dwells in

I wake to think about
your lost and broken beauty
and my speechless love.
Of our embraces I remember
only my own whisperings
and your silence,
and the dead centres
when I arrived at those quiet
terrifying balances where
you never spoke my name.

I ask myself, what
was my hope of us and
what was my intention?
I would have liked simply
to hang by my teeth
from your teeth
on those high wires
that criss-cross the striped
circus of the world.

Or to have swum with you
under the water
among the coloured fish
silent and narrow
where hands and fins
brush under darkness
and where medals of light
decorate champion swimmers.

My sleep in your arms
did never awaken you,
my staring at the noble
mask of your face
did never make it live,
and I thought to myself:
what magnificence,
carved and ancient.

This and the shape
of your ear is what
stays in my mind, pictures
that tremble and change,
like what is left over
after a visit to a
breathtaking exhibition
in the museum of a foreign country.

Winter one

Your burning image
       is buried in the mirror
of a hotel room in a winter city
       with *go lovely rose,*
        myself in Egypt
on cold and pathless deserts
       where the wind
destroys horizons and blinds
       the wanderer.

I open no letters
       but I think
this snowless yearless day
of ancient countless kings
       torn from history,
of Aramaic profiles widespaced eyes
and voices falling
       from the darkness
like flowers
       (a world's ivory
atoms in galleries of bone,
Egyptian light and sand
blowing against the eyes
dyking uneasy speech).

Words move like air:
       smoke dragons,
they uncoil their breath of fire;
       my silence mimes
the dragon's endless dance
       and slowly
the truth of falling stars
slides from the mirror.

My tongue
      dissolves to visions:
white cities rise
      from swanskin coverlets;
lightstreaked
      your sleep encloses to contain
the rose and all its causes
      while down pillows
harden with the dawn,
      and pillars of the heart
are turned to stone.

Remembering you

When you kissed you
kissed like a young man
filled with greeting and gaiety;

when you loved you
loved like an old man
filled with slowness and ceremony;

when you left you
left like a man of no age
filled with fear that ceremony

had given me something
to keep more lasting than ritual
richer and brighter than darkness.

Goodbye song

Someday some woman
is going to kill you
for that expression
on your face, don't
worry it won't be
me, I'm not one of
the killing kind

instead I die into
your moated eye
when you stand
saying goodbye,
extinguished, ash-
dead, a scattering
of snow, and when

she that woman
does turn around
someday just when
you have that same
goodbye look and
she kills you, man
unmanned and buoy-
ant at last will you

fall a blurry star
into the lap of sky-
gazers, will you stand
a stem with the flower
broken in the vase
of winter or be a
wall of snow against
the night, no I am

the crumbling star
the blurred goodbye,
the unwon wall of
winter spring never
leaps over, I am
the promise with the
flower broken, I am
your speech and so
your echoing No

that the uniform
come-and-go of the
solitary policeman
on his beat does
not even sound the
depth, or know the
death in which we
part, nor can he see
the point of morning
where we never meet.

Saints and others

I'll write no more poems,
I'll love no man.
I'll live in tall Toronto
where it rains against the sun,
here saints are very many
but I am not one.

I was once proud and
loved myself, I lived
five thousand feet
above sea level, loved
my prairie city and the wild
windscattered rose
and no-one read the sky
so clear so true as I.

In summer I travelled,
I mined the ocean
and shone like Lucifer,
talked with fish, stacked
sunsets like poker chips.
I loved myself and loved
the great seabirds
and the cool dark places
under their wingspread
I loved the eyeblue waters
which opened to my hand.

What now my human thirst?
seadeep; and my love hunger?
drowned; what of the saints?
they live in the wide world.
I live in tall Toronto
where it rains against the sun,
and saints there may be many
but I am not one.

My love of birds has flown
no wing now stirs the sky
the fires I lit are dead.
Extinguished Lucifer
stagnates and lies alone
under the rotting pier;
he dreams of sunlit hell
and the sea is his blind eye,
my hand his fist of stone.

So we were noble; like the Titanic
we sank and slept alone;
who knows what voyages await
drowned travellers like us?
I dream I am the wild windscattered rose, the parting
waters but wake to traffic noise.
Ruined and glorious
I make my soapbox speech
where no-one hears me;
it is no use.
I'm my dishonoured brother,
my hand his fist of stone.

Desert stone

From out of our
dwellings have I heard
the voices call
and from the locked
mountain have I heard
the voices and from
the burning nest
in the desert from

the driest reaches
have I carried
the seeds of fire
and placed them
in a nest of fire
and my face was
lighted by the dark
the waiting waters.

In our tents
extinguished were
the nests of fire
and in our tents
blighted were
the seeds of light
and to the desert wind
ravenous
as a burning lion
we awoke.

And you said:
Miriam make dance
the desert stone;
and I answered:
blind Moses younger
brother who sailed
through seas of grass
to autumn pyramids,
I said: from the
buried heart of
Miriam you have
struck the bitter
waters:

I will bathe the feet
of salty wanderers
until they lift and dance
upon the desert stone,
and all my tears will fall
upon the desert stone,
until my tears will melt
the world of desert stone.

Looking for
strawberries in June

I have to tell you
about the words I
used to know, such
words, so sheer, thin
transparent, so light
and quick, I had such
words for wind for
whatever grew
I knew a certain
leaf-language from
somewhere, but now

it is all used up
I have come to the
end of some line or
other like walking
on railroad ties in
the country looking
for strawberries in
June and suddenly
the ties end in the
middle of no-place
and I stop to look
around to take my
direction but I

don't recognize the
landscape. It is all
grey, feathery, the
voices of birds are
foreign, yet I used
to know such words
japanned, brushed and
papery, whitefolded

Russian flowerwords
cabbage roses, huge
holes in the head of
the universe pouring
out rosy revolutions:

and I used to know
swarthy eastern words
heavy with Hebrew, then
I was kidnapped by
gypsies, I knew the
up and down of their
dark-blue anger, the
leathery touch of
the fortune-telling
begging wandering
words, but what's
become of them?
I don't know, I'm

just standing here
on the threshold of
a different country,
everything is made
of plastic and silence;
what month is it any-
way? I'm knocking at
the door but nobody
answers. I mutter *Lenin
Karl Marx, Walt Whitman
Chaucer, Hopkins,* even
Archibald Lampman, but
nobody comes, I don't

know the password
I only know it has
nothing to do with
being good or true
nothing to do with
being beautiful.

Summer letters

All the postmen
in the world es-
pecially the swarth-
y-faced one who
crossed in front
of my car just
now what do
they think about
as they deliver
their letters all
over the world?

Here where our
flag has a red
maple leaf on
a white ground
they wear blue un-
iforms and peaked
caps and this one
the swarthy-skinned
one was young but
he wasn't think-
ing about king Ead-
mund's head or Ael-
fric's homilies he
never had to study
anglo-saxon to de-
liver his letters
never had to worry
about king Ael-
fred's many-oared
ships or the old
monks carefully

writing out poems
in manuscripts that
would some day be
collected in museums.

And here as he
crosses the street
he is not concerned
about how to dis-
pose space in a
city block or how
to enclose Paul
Klee in a yellow
wash of sun on
the Saskatchewan
prairie he's
lucky he doesn't
care he's lucky
he's too young
to measure the
cold air sound-
ing in music.

And he's lucky
he's too young to
wonder is there any-
thing in nature
makes these hard
hearts he's so
lucky he has
no dead letters
in his mailbag
addressed to ealdor-
man Byrhtnoth or
to king Lear or to
any other lost
civilization.

Of course he knows
people still live
in the ruins
right here in
this lovely city
right here behind
the old hospital
right here on
Mutual street but
he's lucky these
ruins are all num-
bered so he can
deliver the let-
ters and know
what is for whom
and for where.

And think about
going home at
three o'clock and
not of fighting the
Danes and think
about taking his
shoes off at
three o'clock and
not about the al-
legiance he owes
his lord and
think about listen-
ing after supper when
all the letters have
been delivered
to the long mind-
less mutated song
of the lawnmower
and not to the
sound of gold rings
as they ghostly
fall from the hands
of those longdead
treasure-givers.

Ukrainian church

Little father your
rhythmic black robe
against white snow
improvises you
a black note
on a white keyboard

let me follow
into your churchbarn
through the gate
to the onion domes
where your carrot
harvest burns
a fire of candles

let me follow
in the cool light
as you move through
God's storehouse
as you put the bins
in order as you set
each grain in place

let me follow
as your voice
moves through the
familiar liturgy
to the low caves
of Gregorian chant
and let me hear
little father

how you pray
for all your geese
for the cow fertile
at Easter, and the
foundations of new
houses to be strong
and firmly set

and let me hear
how you beseech
for all your people
a clear road, an
open gate and
a new snowfall
fresh, dazzling
white as birchbark

My travels

I have looked at
beautiful things
in the museums of
foreign countries
all over the world
and I can report
they are still
mourning for Christ
on the tapestries
of Bucharest while
in Moscow the gold
icons are blazing
with the intense
motherhood of dark
medieval madonnas.

On the mountains
of new Jerusalem
in a house of
glass and stone
I read in a broken
alphabet the deed
of sale written
in the hand of
my forefather Bar
Kochba a brave
warrior and later
on the cliffs of
Jaffa (spelled Joppa)
an old papyrus
dating from the
time of Rameses
the Second warned
me what may befall
the traveller in a
strange country:
thou dost sleep
for thou art worn
out a coward steals
thy bow thy sheath-
knife and thy quiver
thy reins are cut
in the darkness
thy weapons are
become dry land.

And from Warsaw
where I went much
later I can report
that the war is not
over yet the stones
of the ghetto still
whisper at night
the old city cries
from the cellars
the Vistula moans,
the music of summer
hides nothing in
Warsaw on Saturday
afternoons when the
Lazienki Park is
empty and Chopin
is dead and I study
the clever walls
of the Satirical
Café in the Square
of the Three Crosses.

And in Hamburg
I discover the
Germans are still
hating the Jews and
in Kiel the same
and in the quiet
gardens of Munich
still the same, it
was no pleasure
being a Jew in
Bucharest I did
not mention it to
anyone in Moscow

I softpedalled it
in Warsaw while
in Jerusalem where
everyone is some
kind of Jew or
other it was no
pleasure either:
thou dost sleep
for thou art worn
out a coward steals
thy bow thy sheath-
knife and thy quiver
thy reins are cut
in the darkness
thy weapons fall
to the ground
thy weapons are
become dry land.

I am homesick I
am packing up
I am going home
but now I don't
know anymore
where home is.

Love poem

I will swallow your
eyes and leave only
pools of darkness.

I will take the words
from your mouth and leave
only lakes of stillness.

Attend to my miracle
I am kissing your body
making it white as stone.

The pools and lakes
of your eyes and mouth
the white stone

Of your body will
make a labyrinth
of fabled cities

And a marbled palace
of many rooms where
the whole world

Will be glad to pay
admission to wander
through the many rooms

To look at my
miracle pools and soft
monuments until

At last the whole world
will go to sleep happy
at eight o'clock

Under a soft white fleece.

Camping

Walking through the unlanterned
darkness, returning to the starcold
glacier of myself after a time
in the hot sun, through
the tree branches looking up
and seeing the stillness
and feeling its edges against my ribs,
I shiver and empty my pocket of stones.

The stones fall to the ground
beside the extinguished fire
and the flap of the tent
rustles in the wind;
yesterday's rain
still falls from the leaves
and I hardly look at the stones.

I look at the dark hollow hole
that waits
patiently for me to return
silent in its knowledge
perfect in its shape
bell-clear in its sound and
unerring in its cold sources
which are my own sources.

The glass trumpet

1
A rainwet road
on some empty-
hearted night,
myself an empty
carton for the
world to stuff
death into,
or a flimflam-
sy frame for

the map of man-
itoba or any
birthplace, a
carton for car
wheels to run
over (one way
of reducing
three dimensions
to two because

force never en-
larges is always
reductive or haven't
you ever noticed
the flatness of
folded cartons?)
one way of return-
ing to earth all
you lost icelandic

eagles immobile
and dew-covered,
all you tired heb-
rew squirrels nut-
hoarding saints,

and you, gimli, my
love-place my most
lake-washed, always
pink in a summer

of always dark
evergreens and al-
ways souvenired
with winter and
the winter escapers,
the poor dying out
cottage dwellers
always such pure
sinners at the

poisoned wells al-
ways such wanderers
on roads choked with
dust and cherries
and always the gold-
en buffalo impaled
on license plates
burning burning
away the sunsets.

2
These creatures
all outside the map
outside this empty-
hearted night of
rain who live be-
yond this grief
of world will be
the grainy sand
to make sweet

your mouths and
they will be
the breath of all
who died to make
sweet your mouths
of all who died
to give you breath
unbittered, so you
blow always in the

giant cauldrons
of this turning
world the sand
they gave to make
sweet your mouths,
they blow such
swantailed glass
as gabriel awaits
to trumpet out

the joyous news
of the high eagle
nested, squirrels
asleep, cartons
walled, wells pur-
ified, and prairies
dark with herds
of living un-
metallic buffalo.

3

The glass trumpet
blows no miracles
but sings the last
of death and loss
and the farthest
rim revealed, the
empty night fills
with our gone voices
and the rain, and
the glass trumpet

blows, it tells
of maps and sand
and people number-
less on numbered
city streets and
then it tells of
our blind sick-
ness healed and
holds us open-eyed
in pure transparency.

The lonely love of middle age

From the garish palazzo and
the city's heaving sea of light
the lamps shine with bravura and
the lonely love of middle age.

The many-layered ships
of the highrise buildings
sway in the wind, are sharp
and thin as knife cuts

in the landscape of steel are
sharp as the graze of thorns
on my outer eye which
remembers that somewhere

under its transparencies
floats my inner eye and
under it another eye the
earliest of all, it sees

somewhere in a neglected
field the beards of milkweed
and the shells of dry old men
and remembers how the wind

riffles through your grey hair
with fading laurel leaves
and I see with all my
many eyes how your eyes

are dark as almond hearts
and smooth as the inside
of almond shells, how they
are filled with the years

bitter and stormy that
you buried long ago deep
in the earth, how your
eyes have travelled far

beyond the starry touch
of any young ghost
and how under the lamp your
eyes still shine with bravura

the lonely love of middle age.

A song of North York
between Sheppard and Finch

Go out and be redeemed by morning
scooped and hollowed out and
filled with sun; the world
was ravined by night and now
divides to township roads
where daylight comes to join
each bare and hummocked field
to its closest neighbour field
while the sky's bluecornered clips
fasten the clouds of light
into a large still photograph.

Begin at nine, the stroke of your salvation
and the whole world opens
its secret drawer of spring;
all North York assaults
my rattling window;
the shabby wind blows
up a smell of gasoline
and parking meters shine
like newly coined teenagers
while the red mail trucks
fly past on Yonge street
gay as greeting cards
sent out by fortune.

New Year's Day

I have no words
for my heart
only heavy, and
an old age and
another new year

when I open the door
to my empty house
I leave the snow-
fall outside, the
starpoints of

white quiet and
all the north
and inside in
the darkness I
close my eyes

squeeze them tight
and look, a million
little gold stars
are falling and
look, my old age

here in the dark-
ness is whirling
and flying with the
little gold stars
and look, my old age
is dancing

Driving home

Classic ESSO
             bloodlit SHELL
signs
     omens
            mysteries
on daylight roads
            look at them hang
conchy
     paunchy worlds
drunken planets
     insane balloons
electric lovecharms
            dangling
from sunlit skies
            (don't shout
my name, whisper it)
            I'm coming
driving to the Volga
            on the world throughway
past the grain elevators
            through Levitan's
painted nights
            to his charcoal beaches
driving from Winnipeg
            to Chekhov's nineteenth-century
consumption
            in the swampy summers
outside of Moscow, driving to
Stanislavsky, his wild-eyed strike
for future, act of the new

And there's my grandfather's mill
                  beside the marshy road
in the village Hitler burned
and there's my grandfather
                  with his flourdusty beard
printer's-ink-smell of books
                  and my mother running
barefoot
      in a forest of birches,
                        she's a force
on fire with rage
                  with joy
and here's my father
                  building an arbour
in our backyard in the
                        new world
coming in with
                  his Sunday cucumbers
                  and here's me
with my firstborn
                  running after his
gesturing arms
                  never catching him
and here's my second son
                  placid smiling
                        (deceptive)
and here's my English husband
                  stepping out of the picture

Classic ESSO
            geometric oracle
lined, circled, and
            alphabeted
monoyellow moonyellow
            SHELL
(transformed lyre)
            poet's cymbal
culture flag
            against billboard hangovers
programmed lovecharm
            (don't tell me
it doesn't work
            it works, but
you have to ask the right questions)

Colours hang heavy
            heavy over my head
what shall this person do?
            this person
shall be a captive
            a seal in a park zoo
asleep under the water
            a passenger in a
locked car or a camel
            in the city's compound
shedding its hair
            in a northern country;
and this person
            shall be a prophet
wake all the dead rabbis
                of Lithuania
take dictation from them
            plan strictness of study
how
    not to forget

And this person
            shall be a singer
journey forth
            when night falls
when the temple voices
            rise thin
                tenorous
above the rafters
            when the gates are open

(Don't shout
            my name, whisper it
to the world's rivers)
            I'm coming
Father Volga
            wait for me
                Mother Assiniboine
I'm coming
            through the Northwest Passage
from east of Labrador where
            the arctic birds
are folding
            their daylight feathers
between sky and earth
            in cold lullabies,
where the blacksmith
            of all possibilities
is thundering
            stoking his furnace
for a new kind of people

The mosquitoes rise
                in clouds
celestial
        ESSO
                ambiguous
                        SHELL
the traffic roars
                in the mirror
tells me
        I am on my way home;
                home?
Fool
        you *are* home
                you were home
in the first place
                and
if you don't look out
                it's going to be
now this minute
                classic ESSO
                        bloodlit SHELL
forever

Green world two

Locked in a glassy iceland lake
I was a child chinning myself
on reflected treetops.
Into my green world
winter shone and splashed
me fresh with light.

My summer gone
the knob of light still turns
in that locked lake;
under the seal of ice
the cabined light still burns
and the yellow haystacks flare
on underwater beaches.
Far above the snow
fills the falling world
to its topmost branches.

Icons

Suddenly
in middle age
instead of withering
into blindness
and burying myself
underground
I grow delicate
and fragile
superstitious;
I carry icons
I have begun
to worship
images.

I take them out
and prop them up
on bureau tops
in hotel rooms
in Spain
I study them
in locked libraries
in Leningrad
I untie them
from tourist packages
in Italy
they warm me
in the heatless winters
of London in the
hurry-up buses
of Picadilly.

My icons are not
angels or holy
babies they have
nothing to do
with saints or
madonnas, they
are mostly of
seashores summer
and love which I no
longer believe in
but I still believe
in the images,
I still preserve
the icons:

a Spanish factory
worker talks to me
in a street behind
the cathedral he
offers me *un poco
amor*, the scars on
his hand, his wounded
country and the black-
jacketed police; he
touches me on the
arm and other places,
and the alcoholic
in the blazing square
drinks brandy, confides
that fortunes can still
be made in Birmingham
but he has a bad
lung is hard of
hearing and owns
an apartment in Palma.

In Montreal a man
in a white shirt
with his sleeves
rolled up is reading
a book and waiting
for me in a room
with the door ajar,
the light falls
through the open
door the book
falls from his
open hand and he
stands up and
looks at me with
open eyes.

Of course I know
these are only
icons; there is
no such thing
as love left in
the world but
there is still
the image of it
which doesn't let
me wither into
blindness which
doesn't let me
bury myself
underground which
doesn't let me
say yes to the
black leather police
or the empty libraries
or the lonely rooms
or the foggy windows
of cold London buses.

The world is getting
dark but I carry
icons, I remember
the summer
I will never forget
the light.

Pont Mirabeau in Montreal

What happened to
Apollinaire's Pont
Mirabeau, to his nos-
talgic *sonne l'heure*
and *je demeure*; we
transported it to
Montreal's Lafontaine
Park and every Sunday
we walk there in a
jungle of birds, French
words, we stand on his
Pont Mirabeau, throw
popcorn to the swans,
eat peanuts, watch the
bicycle racers receive
kisses from their girls
ribbons from the mayor,
nobody needs to translate
anything anymore, every
gesture is international,
with the Pont Mirabeau
we have changed the locale
of the world, now every
city intersects us.

The season's lovers

In the daisied lap of summer
the lovers lay, they dozed
and lay in sun unending
they lay in light they slept
and only stirred
each one to find the other's lips.
At times they sighed
or spoke a word
that wavered on uneven breath,
he had no name and she forgot
the ransomed kingdom of her death.

When at last the sun went down
and chilly evening stained the fields
the lovers rose and rubbed their eyes:
they saw the pale wash of grass
heighten to metallic green
and spindly tongues of granite mauve
lick up the milk of afternoon
they gathered all the scattered light
of daisies to one place of white
and ghostly poets lent their speech
to the stillness of the air
the lovers listened, each to each.

Into the solid wall of night
the lovers looked, their clearer sight
went through that dark intensity
to the other side of light.
The lovers stood, it seemed to them
they hung upon the world's rim—
he clung to self, and she to him;
he rocked her with his body's hymn
and murmured to her shuddering cry
you are all states, all princes I,
and sang against her trembling limbs
nothing else is, he sang, *but I.*

They lifted the transparent lid
from world false and world true
and in the space of both they flew.
He found a name, she lost her death
and summer lulled them in its lap
with a leafy lullaby.
There they sleep unending sleep
the lovers lie
he with a name, she free of death
in a country hard to find
unless you read love's double mind
or invent its polar map.

The eight-sided white barn

I know now for whom
I was saving that eight-
sided white barn at the
corner of Dufferin and
Steeles Avenue, every time
I passed it the morning
would shiver and dance
and I wanted to frame
it all into a poem so

I have just given you
an eight-sided white barnboat and it has a ramp
(or gangplank) in front
of it for the animals
to come in on and it
has a turret on top
of it for someone to
gaze out of and see
the dove, the leaf, and
the lay of the land

and it has a field
around it, full of
ploughed-up earthen
waves crowned with the
foam of snow, and
the blown straw of
Toronto's skimpy winter
and it has an endlessly
unrolling slapdash table-
cloth sky, stained with
wind, blown by rain
covering everything.

Between the plangent sky
and the ploughing sea in
the sun-ice of Ontario on
the snowish shield of the
brittle world we are land-
ploughers, nightskaters
we are seafarers in the
flood who journey out
in a barnboat to touch
the broken leaf, to hear
the dove, to brush through
the boundaries of what-
ever keeps us from being
the wide new world.

The journeying

Trapped in such a paradise
(old Adam in a stuffy lair)—
pity the guilty self again;
my own last soul at mercy's end
begins once more the journeying.
Cell has starved from cell
and fallen from the bone,
body becomes a part again
and sloughs the dying whole.

Alive I burn: and burn beyond
archaic wastes of total snow,
no winter bird can sing the mean
of distance between yes and no,
or beast asleep can wake to know
if part can live apart from whole:
no man, no talking fish can tell
whose death will fire the heaven-slow-
time-blackened chimneys of the soul.

Waking

Love
remember me
as I do you our
locked voices and the
morning mists over
the city how
we hung in the
transparent bell
of summer and
swayed to the
rhythm of an
accordion-folded
sun

Canadians

Here are
our signatures:
geese, fish, eskimo
faces, girl-guide
cookies, ink-drawings
tree-plantings, summer
storms and winter
emanations.

We look
like a geography but
just scratch us
and we bleed
history, are full
of modest misery
are sensitive
to double-talk double-take
(and double-cross)
in a country
too wide
to be single in.

Are we real or
did someone invent
us, was it Henry
Hudson Etienne Brûlé
or a carnival
of village girls?
Was it
a flock of nuns
a pity of indians
a gravyboat of
fur-traders, professional

explorers or those
amateur map-makers
our Fathers
of Confederation?

Wherever you are
Charles Tupper Alexander
Galt Darcy McGee George
Cartier Ambrose Shea
Henry Crout Father
Ragueneau Lord Selkirk
and John A.—however
far into northness
you have walked—
when we call you
turn around please and
don't look so
surprised.